SMART PORTS IN THE PACIFIC

NOVEMBER 2020

ASIAN DEVELOPMENT BANK

 Creative Commons Attribution 3.0 IGO license (CC BY 3.0 IGO)

© 2020 Asian Development Bank
6 ADB Avenue, Mandaluyong City, 1550 Metro Manila, Philippines
Tel +63 2 8632 4444; Fax +63 2 8636 2444
www.adb.org

Some rights reserved. Published in 2020.

ISBN 978-92-9262-427-9 (print); 978-92-9262-428-6 (electronic); 978-92-9262-429-3 (ebook)
Publication Stock No. TCS200293-2
DOI: http://dx.doi.org/10.22617/TCS200293-2

The views expressed in this publication are those of the authors and do not necessarily reflect the views and policies of the Asian Development Bank (ADB) or its Board of Governors or the governments they represent.

ADB does not guarantee the accuracy of the data included in this publication and accepts no responsibility for any consequence of their use. The mention of specific companies or products of manufacturers does not imply that they are endorsed or recommended by ADB in preference to others of a similar nature that are not mentioned.

By making any designation of or reference to a particular territory or geographic area, or by using the term "country" in this document, ADB does not intend to make any judgments as to the legal or other status of any territory or area.

This work is available under the Creative Commons Attribution 3.0 IGO license (CC BY 3.0 IGO) https://creativecommons.org/licenses/by/3.0/igo/. By using the content of this publication, you agree to be bound by the terms of this license. For attribution, translations, adaptations, and permissions, please read the provisions and terms of use at https://www.adb.org/terms-use#openaccess.

This CC license does not apply to non-ADB copyright materials in this publication. If the material is attributed to another source, please contact the copyright owner or publisher of that source for permission to reproduce it. ADB cannot be held liable for any claims that arise as a result of your use of the material.

Please contact pubsmarketing@adb.org if you have questions or comments with respect to content, or if you wish to obtain copyright permission for your intended use that does not fall within these terms, or for permission to use the ADB logo.

Corrigenda to ADB publications may be found at http://www.adb.org/publications/corrigenda.

Notes:
In this publication, "$" refers to United States dollars.

On the cover: Tonga port container upgrade under ADB's Nuku'alofa Port Upgrade Project (photo by ADB).

Contents

Table and Figures	iv
Foreword	v
Acknowledgments	vi
Abbreviations	vii
Executive Summary	viii
1 Introduction	**1**
2 Smart Ports Literature Review	**2**
2.1 What Is a Smart Port?	2
2.2 Evolution of the Smart Ports Concepts	3
2.3 Pathway to Smart Port Maturity	6
2.4 Examples of Smart Port Initiatives Worldwide	15
3 Relevance of Smart Ports Concept to the Pacific	**21**
3.1 Regional Characteristics	21
3.2 Port Operational Characteristics	22
3.3 Applicability of Smart Ports Concepts	24
4 Smarter Ports Development Framework	**26**
4.1 Regional Mission and Vision	26
4.2 Smarter Ports Thematic Strategies	28
5 Getting Started	**36**
5.1 Crucial Takeaways	36
5.2 Tangible Short- and Medium-Term Strategies	37
5.3 Key Considerations in Implementation	38

Table and Figures

TABLE

Observations per Visited Port   23

FIGURES

1	Industry 4.0	3
2	Maturity Levels for a Smart Port	7
3	3D Model of Jetty Prepared in Building Information Modeling Environment	8
4	Performance Dashboard	9
5	Geographical Data Visualization	10
6	Simulation of Terminal Operations	13
7	Digital Twin in Logistics Industry	14
8	Port Community Portal Concept	16
9	Digital Twin Concept	18
10	Lock Gate Monitoring (Live Data Visualization)	18
11	Closed-Circuit Television Analytics	19
12	Four Themes of the Smart Ports Mission Statement for the Pacific	27
13	Quick Wins and Longer-Term Strategies	37

Foreword

Maritime trade is an essential lifeline for the remote island nations of the Pacific. The Pacific developing member countries (DMCs) of the Asian Development Bank (ADB) rely almost entirely on imports for essential goods—including food, fuel, and medicine—and many are working to develop their export economies as key drivers of growth. However, existing trade infrastructure and processes in the Pacific DMCs are outdated, inefficient, and vulnerable to natural hazards and the effects of climate change.

These challenges contribute to safety and security risks, alongside the exceptionally high costs of goods, services, and doing business in the region. The coronavirus pandemic is placing additional strain on the maritime transport sector—with reduced shipping volumes threatening commercial performance and intensifying the need to improve port efficiency.

Smart ports leverage technology and improved business processes to maximize the use of space, time, money, and natural resources—contributing to greater operational and energy efficiency, heightened safety and security, and improved environmental sustainability. Modernizing maritime trade with appropriate smart port features can help the Pacific DMCs to address key risks, reduce the costs of goods and services, and drive economic growth.

ADB is supporting its Pacific DMCs to improve trade logistics, build resilience to external shocks, and deepen regional cooperation and integration. This study was commissioned as a part of ADB's regional technical assistance, *Trade and Transport Facilitation in the Pacific*. The technical assistance was designed to analyze trade and transport dynamics in the region, and to identify investment pathways to support the Pacific DMCs in capitalizing on new growth opportunities.

This study examines the practical applications of smart ports in the Pacific context. It explores options to align international best practices with unique local features, such as relatively small trade volumes, geographic isolation, and vulnerability to extreme weather events. The study makes recommendations on how to achieve short-term "wins" by implementing technology and business process solutions, and provides a strategic framework for developing more robust smart port ecosystems over time.

The study is intended to foster dialogue among governments and development partners on how to leverage smart ports to support trade, resilience, and more inclusive economic growth across the region.

Leah C. Gutierrez
Director General
Pacific Department
Asian Development Bank

Acknowledgments

This publication was commissioned by the Asian Development Bank, under the regional technical assistance for *Trade and Transport Facilitation in the Pacific* (RETA 8674). The Government of Japan financed the technical assistance on a grant basis, through the Japan Fund for Poverty Reduction. The Asian Development Bank wishes to acknowledge the valuable inputs and contributions of all stakeholders that contributed to this piece.

Bas van Dijk (Director for Maritime Asia Pacific Region and Smart Ports Expert, Royal HaskoningDHV) prepared the publication, with inputs and under the overall guidance of Alexandra Pamela Chiang (Senior Transport Specialist, Transport Sector Group, Sustainable Development and Climate Change Department) and Cha-Sang Shim (Transport Specialist, Pacific Department). Dong Kyu Lee (Director, Transport Division, Pacific Department) provided support and direction while preparing the publication, and Mary France Rull Creus (Associate Project Analyst, Pacific Department) provided technical assistance administration support. Cecilia Caparas and Raymond De Vera (Knowledge Management Officers) managed the production process.

Abbreviations

ADB	-	Asian Development Bank
BIM	-	building information modeling
CCTV	-	closed-circuit television
DMC	-	developing member country
IoT	-	Internet of Things
IT	-	information technology
RFID	-	radio-frequency identification
SOP	-	standard operating procedure
TEU	-	twenty-foot equivalent unit
TGS	-	TEU ground slots
TOS	-	terminal operating system

Executive Summary

This report explores the applicability of the smart ports concept in the Pacific region, taking into account unique features of the relatively small throughput volumes of Pacific ports, the region's geographic remoteness from international markets, and its vulnerability to extreme weather conditions that disrupt port operations occasionally.

According to Port Technology International, a smart port is one that ensures "no waste of space, time, money and natural resources."[a] The concept of smart ports involves harnessing advanced technologies to enhance port operational efficiency, energy efficiency, and environmental sustainability.

However, this vision is tempered with practical limitations. It is unrealistic to expect all ports to achieve an ultimate smart port level of maturity and sophistication overnight. The transformation toward a smart port is gradual, comprising incremental steps. This evolutionary process can be subdivided into the following five steps:

1. Data capture
2. Collaboration
3. Decision support
4. Learning
5. Digital transformation

Considering the specific characteristics of the Pacific, some of the effective smart port solutions in other parts of the world may not work in the region mainly due to cargo volumes that do not justify large investments in information technology (IT) systems or equipment. However, this limitation does not imply that ports in the Pacific cannot be made smarter. On the contrary, solutions to improve trade efficiency and port operations produce positive returns. Solar or wind energy can be easily implemented to reduce the environmental footprint, e.g., with LED lighting for the terminals. While large-scale automation may not be a realistic option, the implementation of digital systems to measure performance and identify bottlenecks contributes to efficient and cost-effective port operations, especially in the Pacific context.

The Pacific region has unique challenges when it comes to climate change and natural hazards such as typhoons, earthquakes, and tsunamis. These events lead to disruption of vessel traffic and significantly impact the reliability of the logistics chain. With accurate weather data and prediction models based on artificial intelligence, port authorities can be alerted promptly to potential threats to the port and its operations, allowing for better mitigation measures and enhancement of emergency preparedness.

---

[a] Port Techology, 2016. What is a Smart Port? Olaf Merk, Administrator for Ports and Shipping, ITF, OECD.

Initial field visits were conducted at the following ports to assess smart ports potential in the Pacific:

- Queen Salote International Wharf in the Kingdom of Tonga.
- Honiara Port in Solomon Islands.
- Suva Port in the Republic of Fiji.

The key challenges are summarized as follows:

- Low level of digital maturity.
- Lack of written standard operating procedures.
- Reactive vessel planning.
- Customs and quarantine operations exacerbating the bottleneck.
- Limited planned maintenance.
- Occupational safety hazards.

Since the smart ports concept is relatively new and one that has been more established in ports of more developed countries, this report serves two main purposes. First, it seeks to enhance general awareness of such emerging technology. Second, it encourages the piloting of new concepts to apply their potential benefits to ports in less-developed regions. A smart ports development framework and preliminary guidelines have been provided to decision makers to support smart port initiatives. However, each port is unique and has specific characteristics posing distinctive challenges for its growth and development. Therefore, it is crucial to recognize that this report does not seek to promote a one-size-fits-all approach. The appropriate level of smart port maturity and sophistication should be designed according to the needs and scale of each port.

Smart Ports Mission Statement for the Pacific

"To implement relevant and proven smart technologies in existing ports to improve operational efficiency and business reliability, increase resilience and sustainability, and enhance regional cooperation and integration"

Smart Ports Vision Statement for the Pacific

"To enable a transparent port logistics sector working together as one region and one port community to ensure best value for their customers at a minimum waste of space, time, money, and natural resources"

Smart ports mission and vision statements have been proposed to ensure alignment with the regional decision makers in the Pacific ports sector in terms of investments in technology implementation. This initial proposal can be used as a good starting point to design the smart port initiative and should be adjusted according to the specific needs of each port.

Four broad thematic areas have been identified to support the mission and vision statements, taking into consideration the operational priorities of the Asian Development Bank (ADB) in its Strategy 2030 and the unique development characteristics in the Pacific region:

- Improving operational efficiency and reliability.
- Promoting environmental sustainability.

- Enhancing resilience to climate change and natural hazards.
- Strengthening regional cooperation and integration.

The following starting points are crucial for the successful implementation of the smart ports concept in the Pacific:

- **Strive for appropriate "smartness."** Any port can become smarter. There is no limit in terms of port size for the implementation of smarter solutions. But this does not mean that all ports require the same level of "smartness." The appropriate level of smart port maturity and sophistication should be designed according to the needs of each individual port. The journey to becoming smart is a gradual process of transformation for the port.
- **Start small, think long term.** Although steps to become smarter should be incremental, there should be a clear longer-term plan to make sure that any step taken is in line with the longer-term perspective. One of the pitfalls would be to look at individual smart solutions in isolation, for the biggest results are achieved by integrating smart components into port operations and making them available for all. New partnerships may be needed, and collaboration between port users is crucial to maximizing the results of implementing cybersecurity, digitalization of port operations (including customs and biosecurity), and (semi)automated access to the port. It is recommended to pilot innovations and digital tools at a particular port to demonstrate proof of concept before it is scaled up.
- **Gather data as a priority.** Data are key to developing smarter ports; hence any smart ports strategy should start with data gathering. A multiphase plan for smarter ports should be designed with time-bound milestones to ensure that the right data are collected. The description of the necessary data to be collected at each stage includes procedures for data quality assurance, safe data storage, software and hardware needs, and data collection specifications (including budgets). At this time, the technology of sensors and software systems to utilize the digital twin concept in combination with IT solutions are at a mature stage. Therefore, implementing such technology is far more cost-effective now than it was several years ago.
- **Embrace change management.** As part of introducing new smart technologies into the port operations, reevaluating institutional and management capacity structures in the Pacific will be needed. Technical and management roles will need to evolve. Such change management may also involve strengthening regulatory and legislative frameworks, reinforcing interagency coordination, and enhancing transparency and accountability of the government and port authorities.
- **Promote upskilling.** Even though the smart ports concept is mostly about new technologies, the technical skills of end users are needed not only to operate but also to maintain and improve the new tools and systems in order to ensure their sustainability. The smart ports concept can crucially bring transformational changes to port operations, creating high-value job opportunities in a traditional port industry, which will also help retain talent in the sector.

1. Introduction

This study was commissioned to assess and develop smart ports potential in the Pacific region, taking into account its unique features in terms of geographic remoteness, relatively smaller trade volumes mostly concentrated in the import of goods, and the weather conditions that disturb the logistics occasionally.

Port of Suva is the most extensive and busiest container and general port providing the maritime gateway to Fiji's capital Suva. The Fiji Ports Development Project comprised wharf improvements at the ports of Suva and Lautoka, on the island of Viti Levu, the principal gateways for Fiji's international trade. The project's objectives were to achieve a stable macroeconomic environment; support trade, investment, and private sector development; and enhance the economy's competitiveness through sustained improvements in port productivity.

2. Smart Ports Literature Review

Disclaimer:
The mention of specific companies or products of manufacturers does not imply that they are endorsed or recommended by ADB and Royal HaskoningDHV in preference to others of a similar nature that are not mentioned.

2.1 What Is a Smart Port?

A smart port can be defined as a port that ensures "no waste of space, time, money and natural resources."[1] The port of the future is expected to be 100% electric, local emissions-free, and able to process more goods in less time. However, this vision can be tempered with practical limitations such as unavailability of funds to invest in new technologies. In reality, most ports would not be able to reach an ultimate smart port level of maturity and sophistication overnight. The journey to becoming a smart port typically comprises many steps in a gradual transformation to becoming a smarter port.

The following are drivers for adoption of smart port technology:

- **Operational efficiency.** Using smart technologies to increase productivity will help reduce operational costs and relieve congestion of vessels arriving and/or trucks leaving.
- **Asset management.** Technologies (e.g., sensors) that better monitor structural health or ways in which maintenance requirements can be minimized will result in reduced operational costs.
- **Business resilience.** Tools can be used to strengthen commercial business operations, to invest wisely in crisis management and business continuity, to be responsive to changes in port traffic and customer demands, and to provide robust service continuity (e.g., with cybersecurity) and staff capability and training.
- **Safety and security.** Specialized equipment, technologies, and systems can be applied to take over standard repetitive tasks, which will help increase operations safety. The same principle applies to smart security systems to reduce labor-intensive activities (e.g., container screening).
- **Energy efficiency.** Operational costs and environmental impacts are lessened by being more energy-efficient, particularly with electrification or on-site power generation. Energy efficiency does not mean reduced functionality.

---

[1] Port Technology. 2016. What Is a Smart Port? 26 February. https://www.porttechnology.org/news/what_is_a_smart_port/.

- **Environmental management.** Following international global climate agreements, such as those that came out of the 2015 United Nations Climate Change Conference in Paris, governments at all levels (national, regional, and local) look toward ports to contribute to the reduction of greenhouse gas (GHG) emissions and other air pollutants. Port authorities are, therefore, compelled to adopt strategies toward more environmentally friendly operations.

Successful implementation of smart ports application can contribute to a wide range of benefits for ports and stakeholders, including

- improving customer service,
- enhancing occupational health and safety for port staff and users,
- reducing environmental impacts of port operations,
- becoming a better neighbor,
- boosting operational efficiency, and
- increasing profitability.

2.2 Evolution of the Smart Ports Concepts

The smart ports concept has been heavily influenced by the rise of Industry 4.0 (the Fourth Industrial Revolution) and its confluence with the internet of Things (IoT) (Figure 1).

Industry 4.0 was originally led by the manufacturing industry. Since the First Industrial Revolution in the late 1700s, the discovery of mechanization and steam power propelled the shipping industry, and mass production was made possible. The introduction of computers and automation has enabled substantial efficiencies across industries. Today, we are amid Industry 4.0, a generation of cyber-physical systems bringing together digital, physical, and biological systems to control the full life cycle of the product value chain using big data and artificial intelligence (AI).

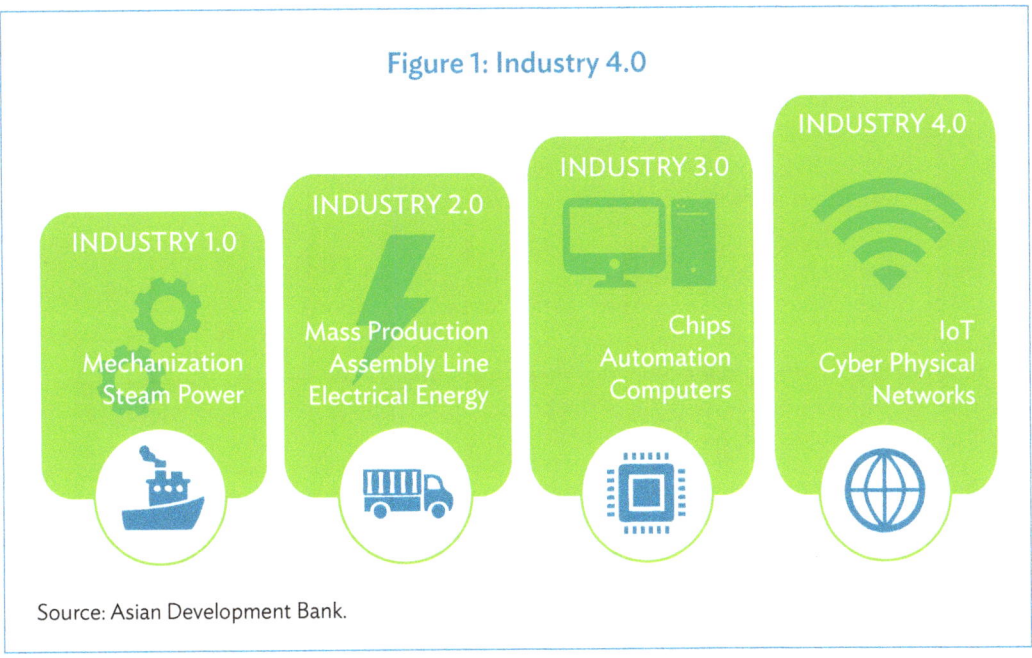

Figure 1: Industry 4.0

Source: Asian Development Bank.

The IoT is a crucial development to interconnect individual computing devices. These devices can "talk" to each other through the internet. The IoT is often described as the concept of connecting physical objects to the internet. These objects will gather data through sensors. With internet connectivity, these data can be sent to cloud systems for storage or computing. Analyzed data can then be transmitted to users or other connected devices for collaboration and decision-making.

Since the port sector is an integral part of a manufacturer's value chain, Industry 4.0 and the IoT have been introduced into the port operations as well, aiming at more efficient operations with less waste of space, time, and resources, resulting in the smart ports concept. The flow of goods in the supply chain is a key focus for smart ports, but the other roles that a port plays can equally benefit from smart initiatives—in asset management, environmental protection, and staff support.

The following are some examples of potential applications:

1. A vessel enters a port and starts berthing.
    a. This terminal and the containers on the vessel make use of IoT technology. All relevant parties will have real-time insight into cargo and vessel arrivals. Human interaction on the ground is highly limited.
    b. With the automated mooring systems, the vessel can berth safely and efficiently.

2. The port equipment is automatically directed to the right location to pick up the containers in the most efficient manner.
    a. The container is scanned with radio-frequency identification (RFID) technology, and data of the container are transmitted to the cloud system.
    b. The cloud analyzes and processes the information and transmits instructions to the port equipment to place the container in the most efficient location within the container yard.

3. The correct truck is loaded with the container and receives the same container data.
    a. At the same time, data of the truck are transmitted to the cloud, which analyzes the performance of the truck. Based on deviations in the performance and the environmental and/or container data, AI systems can estimate the need for maintenance (predictive maintenance).

4. The vessel constantly receives the current status of the freight and can estimate the need to alert its operators when it is time to prepare for leaving the port.
    a. The data are also shared with the port terminal system, which triggers the automated mooring system when approval has been given that the vessel can leave the port.

5. The containers will be shipped to another location or transported to the hinterland.
    a. The cloud system gives an overview of the container locations.
    b. When there is a request for a specific container, the rubber-tired gantry will automatically be directed to the right location to pick up the container and place it on the truck for export from the port. The client of the container will have real-time insight into the location and arrival times.

Thanks to the IoT, ports can operate smarter with a data-driven approach, resulting in better service to clients (vessel operators as well as end users), safer working environment, and higher efficiency.

According to a report by *Forbes*,[2] it is estimated that the IoT will add $10 trillion–$15 trillion to global gross domestic product during 2015–2035 and that "the new rule for the future is going to be, 'Anything that can be connected,' will be connected."

With the wide range of devices connected through the internet and the large amount of data that can be collected, it is becoming increasingly important that the value extracted from the data is maximized. The more value that can be extracted from data, the more efficient and economical the operations associated with that data can be carried out. It is by maximizing the value of data that ports and terminals continue to be competitive. The price of new technologies, such as IoT hardware and software, have declined, signifying that the use of data in port operations has a low-cost but high-positive returns on efficiency and service quality.

To further illustrate, the Port of Rotterdam has identified a step-by-step approach toward a digital port in one of their white papers.[3] Digitization of ports can bring about process efficiencies in and between ports. This efficiency can reap benefits in reduced operational costs, thereby enhancing the competitiveness of individual ports. However, it is not realistic to expect all ports to survive this digitization era. The chance of survival depends on how well the port can share digital information within a system of connected logistics supply chain and ports. The Port of Rotterdam has identified four levels of "digital maturity" for a port cargo community (Figure 2).

- **Level 1: Digitization of individual activities in the port**
  At this level, the individual organizations operating in the port digitize their processes so that they work more efficiently—e.g., by implementing a terminal management system to digitize the administrative and financial processes. Digitalization and automation of the port operations facilitates data collection, which enhances greater cost-efficiencies, safety, and environmental sustainability.
- **Level 2: Integrated systems in a port community**
  Once individual activities in the port have been digitized, the next step in the digital maturity is the digital exchange of information within the port community. This exchange leads to reliable, efficient, and paperless dataflows, resulting in more efficient port operations. The focus in this level is related to securely sharing data. Cybersecurity and cyber resilience are key.
- **Level 3: Logistics chain integrated with hinterland**
  At this level, the hinterland four players (importers, exporters, logistics hubs, domestic transporters) are involved in digital communication with the port community. This integration promotes sharing of real-time information on freight and vessel movements, facilitating better planning.
- **Level 4: Connected ports in the global logistics chain**
  The port and its hinterland connections are extended to other ports around the world, forming a global network of interconnected ports. This network will allow further reductions of inefficiencies in the global logistics chains by optimizing the use of port capacities and achieve shorter, more reliable transit times.

---

[2] J. Morgan. 2014. A Simple Explanation of 'The Internet of Things.' *Forbes*. 13 May.
[3] W. Buck, J. Gardeitchik, and A. van der Deijl. *Move Forward: Step by Step Towards a Digital Port: White Paper*. Port of Rotterdam / British Ports Association. https://www.britishports.org.uk/system/files/documents/smart_port_papers.pdf.

As more IoT-connected devices are introduced to ports and terminals, it is crucial to have a strategy in place to manage the data collected. Companies and organizations may look to appoint a chief information officer, chief digital officer, or similar to help convert the company from a traditional analog business to a digital one. However, to implement a successful digital transformation, there needs to be buy-in across the company with respect to innovation, transformation, agility, and collaboration. Therefore, regardless of whether a company has a chief information officer or chief digital officer, managers and department heads should look at their part of the business and seek ways to improve data collection, storage, analysis, etc. As ports and terminals become more reliant on the use of the internet and electronic information exchange, they also become more vulnerable to cyber threats. A cyberattack could result in disrupted port operations, compromised security, or criminal activities such as theft.

2.3 Pathway to Smart Port Maturity

The process of evolution toward smarter ports can be described in five development stages, as developed by Royal HaskoningDHV:

1. Data capture
2. Collaboration
3. Decision support
4. Learning
5. Digital transformation

Each function in a port organization can be at different levels of smart port maturity and gradually move up the stages as new improvements are made. Some smart concepts can also supersede earlier steps, where perhaps simulation or learning stages are irrelevant. These five stages of smart port maturity are further elaborated in the next paragraphs.

Figure 2 shows the stages of maturity for a port on a mission to become smarter.

Data Capture

Most smart ports concepts rely on data capture, either to validate, justify, and monitor a particular improvement, or to actively feed into a decision-making support or an automated tool. IoT devices capture data with sensors, which can be analyzed with cloud computing. Key to this process is data capture prioritization based on the needs of the port, which is best done through the mapping of the business processes and subsequent identification of the main bottlenecks in the port (e.g., through a digital health check). The focus of the data capture should be on providing supporting information to resolving the main bottlenecks first.

Data capture can range from recording cargo unit numbers and time stamps, to tracking the container dwell time in the port or the crane productivity, to installing sensors to measure structural settlements, to mooring line forces or the amount of trucking loads on block pavement.

The basic data capture can be very simple, but this can become much broader when multiple sources and types of information are gathered, creating a data cloud (warehouse, mine, or lake) or "big data" due to the number of data points acquired. The IoT is the driver for big data management, presenting new and varied data to port clients.

Figure 2: Maturity Levels for a Smart Port

IoT = internet of Things.
Source: Asian Development Bank.

Big data refers to data sets that are too large to be manually managed.[4] The challenges faced when dealing with big data include capturing data, storing data, analyzing data, searching through data, sharing or transferring data, and visualization.

Because of the difficulties associated with extracting value from a large data set, big data has also become synonymous with predictive analytics (footnote 7). This predictive analytics may include an analysis of data sets to find new correlations that can be used to improve productivity. An example for the maritime industry might be data that are collected that relates to mooring line forces, fender forces, vessel motions, environmental conditions, etc., and how this is then analyzed and interpreted to better manage operability and the risk of an incident occurring. Big data can also be used to improve security. For example, surveillance footage collected from hundreds of cameras needs to be analyzed and processed in a way that allows for an early warning system activation.

---

[4] L. Gavrilchik. 2018. *Smart Ports: Intelligent, Sustainable, Relevant.* Royal HaskoningDHV. 31 October. p. 15. https://www.myanmarwaterportal.com/storage/eb/articles/1038/Smart-Ports---leonid.pdf.

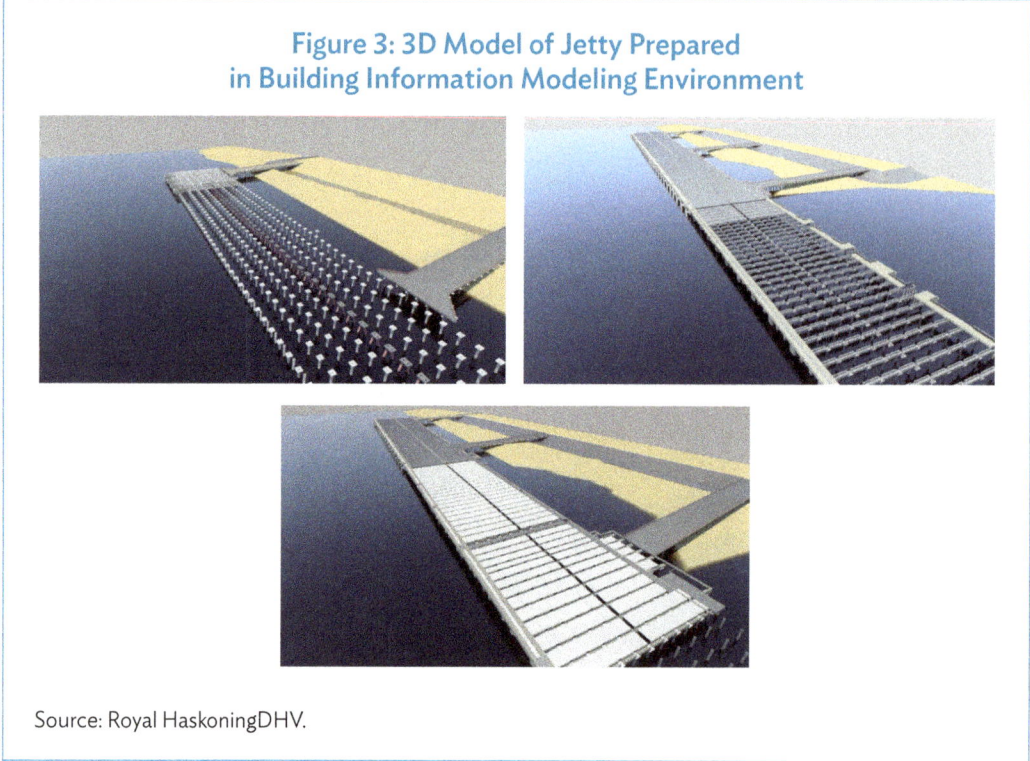

Figure 3: 3D Model of Jetty Prepared in Building Information Modeling Environment

Source: Royal HaskoningDHV.

Data capture should start as early as possible in the design stage (Figure 3). Building information modeling (BIM) is the standard process to ensure that the right information on assets is secured systematically. BIM creates and manages information. The benefits of BIM include better design coordination; improved constructability; and a complete and accurate set of as-built information, which can be fed into the (smart) asset management system.

At the operations level, the ability to capture information from new sources, even in a simple way, can open up options for improved understanding of the behavior of port facilities and support better decision-making. Many port functions are managed based on past practice, experience, and instinct, to which the addition of supporting information (ideally in real time) can guide and shape improved efficiency. These supporting data sets are particularly valuable when the port is expanding or changing use, where the value of past practice is not yet built up.

Digitization is the conversion of manual or paper-based information into an electronically useful format, which is a key element of data capture. This electronically captured data may not be new, but it allows easy onward sharing, analysis, and use within business management. Many ports rely on paper-based information to record events, cargo tallies, equipment maintenance, berthing plans, etc., which have remained broadly unchanged for decades. Paper forms and structures can be built into mobile devices for collecting and centralizing information, often in real time, creating new uses for information to manage the port facility.

The digitization of information is the foundation of any smart port project.

A range of data capture from new sources, sensors, or IoT devices, plus the electronic capture of existing information, forms the base for the next stages of smart port maturity.

Collaboration

The next step in the journey toward a smarter port is the sharing of data and information internally and with clients and other stakeholders. Once information is gathered, value can be extracted from the data in several ways.

Visualize

Managers in ports rely on guidance from systems and information to make decisions, based on short-term performance or planning. The simple ability to manage and display the cloud of data in a meaningful way can support managers in making decisions through a simple dashboard or calendar, or a more complex series of performance metrics (Figure 4). Information can be shown on a geographical map or chart (such as geographic information system), or whatever is needed. Many ports collect data but struggle with the visualization of data into useful forms, which is where flexible and dynamic solutions can really add value (Figure 5). Once information is manipulated into a communicable form, then this can be easily shared, promoting collaboration.

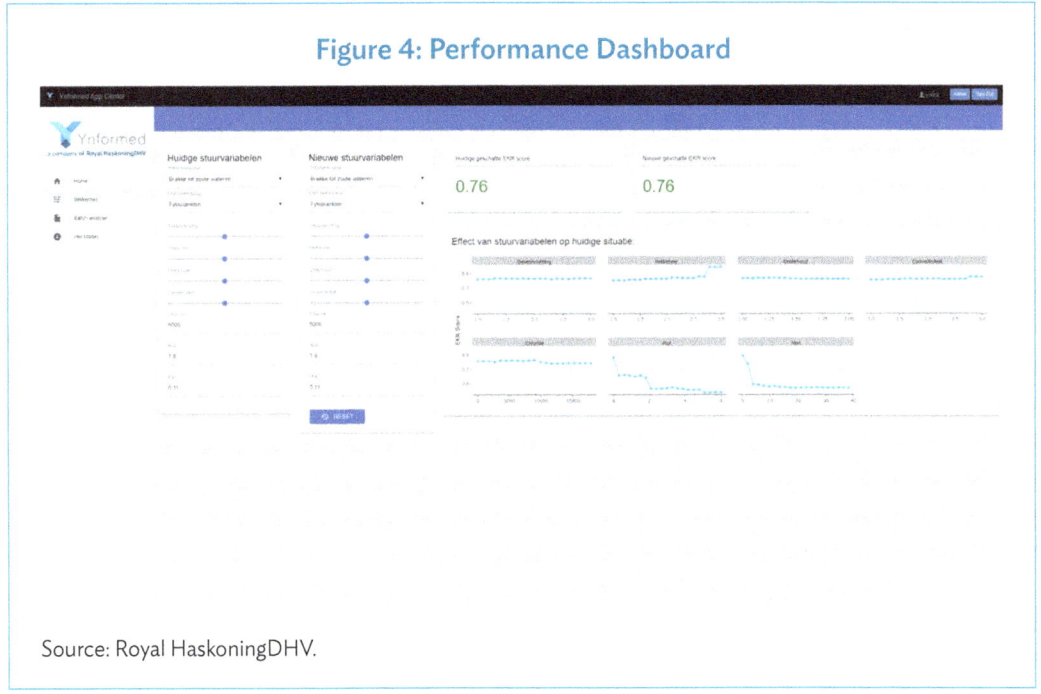

Figure 4: Performance Dashboard

Source: Royal HaskoningDHV.

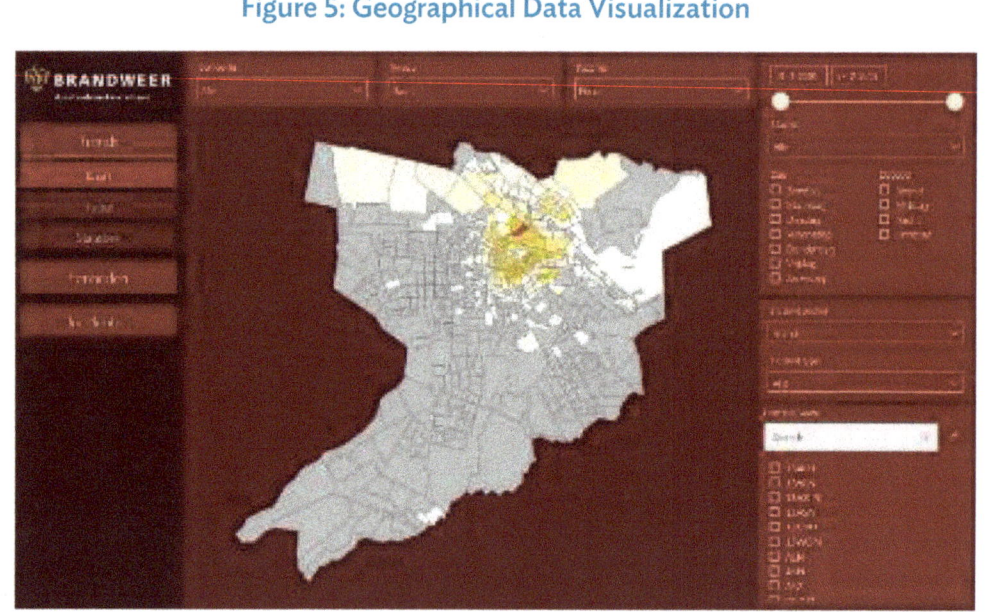

Figure 5: Geographical Data Visualization

Source: The Netherlands Fire Service (Brandweer Nederland).

Share

At a local level, the use of shared information in a port community can promote teamwork. Sharing of process-related information, such as vessel berthing plans, can eliminate communication inefficiency, errors, and knowledge ownership issues that occur at many ports. A data sharing concept in cargo processing, particularly, allows different agencies and port users in the supply chain to plan and react to changes dynamically for the mutual benefits of all. This concept is instinctive in many aspects of port operations, but the use of technology such as port community systems, terminal operating systems (TOSs), and various portals and automated communications can improve efficiency.

At a regional level, sharing of vessel productivity can also be useful, promoting a collective effort to improve overall port performance in the region. The port facility (or terminal) is a service provider within a chain, along with vessel operators, trucking companies, agents, and regulatory bodies. Problems in the logistics chain can usually only be solved by working together on a common goal and vessel productivity transparency could help such a collective effort.

Analyze

The simple visualization and sharing of information can be enhanced greatly by analyzing and organizing to focus on the performance objectives of a particular topic. Data need some interpretation to be relevant for the user to measure against a historical trend, set against a target, or extrapolate to an expected outcome. This is where smart port solutions can start to guide decision-making actively, rather than simply present information for managers to use.

The collaborative state of smart port maturity is focused on technology, but this is the stage where significant business changes (and challenges) exist in breaking down barriers and structures to create more effective communication in the port environment. Technology solutions are tools to support this business evolution.

Decision Support

Smart ports recognize that human planners, managers, and executives have limits to their analytical and decision-making insights across the wide range of functions and detail in a modern port environment. The role of technology tools can go beyond visualizing and presenting information to the staff; it can guide decision-making directly.

At this digitization stage, the data and information are used to guide the staff in making choices on how to deploy resources (people, equipment, energy) and operations (through vessel, trucks, storage) and in optimizing those decisions.

Based on standardized processes and activity steps with defined actors, performance expectations can be set for each function within a port, such as crane lift cycles, truck processing time, invoice production, or machine fuel burn rates.

Historical information captured by sensors or digitization can be used to set performance targets. Thus, real-time performance can be monitored against targets, guiding staff to make decisions with predictable outcomes.

Historical trending and target-setting across many port functions are a useful driver to improve performance, providing a shared focus and boosting service reliability over time as common failings (service delivery reliability) are highlighted and resolved.

The ability to predict performance in a more structured and traceable manner is vital to measure the progress of smart port goals. For example, once the estimated time of arrival for multiple vessels and cargo exchanges is known using predictable quayside productivity and marine services performance, a workable resource schedule and service provision for the period can be produced (daily, weekly). In turn, these predictions guide resource providers (labor, equipment, fuel, maintenance) or supply chain links (distribution centers, truckers, shipping lines) on the vessel calls, expected cargo availability, and expected performance. This simple example is common in most ports and manageable without smart solutions. However, such a system can be expanded to encompass more factors, with many vessel calls, stakeholders, demand for resources, and limitations by weather or supply chain demands coming together to create a demanding picture for management decision-making. Tools that bring together historical and real-time situational data drive better operational decisions to keep the entire organization focused on targets for service quality, resource efficiency, safety, and environmental protection.

Within this broad range of decision-making, system tools can provide detailed guidance on resource and process optimization, such as calculating the need for equipment or staff–skill mix and rostering to make more efficient decisions. This guidance is particularly useful in a flexible labor environment, centered around irregular vessel calls. Within higher-volume environments, specialized systems can provide forecasting and decision support tools to forecast vessel hatch splits, crane production, and equipment movement productivity, as seen in the following image from Jebel Ali Port in the United Arab Emirates.

A port landlord with a vision—who can make decisions on investment in assets or equipment, changing land use, energy efficiency, or differing staff structures—will also benefit from the use of information to guide decision-making. The open-minded analysis of commercial and operational performance can uncover different viewpoints to guide investments and spending in the port, allowing quantifiable value and more accuracy in business case development. Once data are used to guide decisions, then this "learning" on how the port truly behaves and performs in different scenarios in the future is the next stage in smart port maturity.

Port and cargo terminal control room. The room provides visualization and decision support (photo by © Oleg Kozlov / Adobe Stock).

Learn

Once system tools are collecting, visualizing, and sharing data as well as guiding the staff in decision-making in the operation and management of the port, then the information can be used to look ahead for strategic direction of the port by learning how the port can improve.

This can be managed in different ways—in a theoretical simulation or in an actively managed digital twin, both of which offer benefits in managing improvement in the port facility.

Simulation

A simulation tool can recreate the physical, procedural, and resource capability of the port and allow scenario testing to try out new situations that are impractical for the port to do in reality. This experimentation can lead to new efficiencies or new ways to accommodate cargo and adopt new terminal layouts or working practices. Using parameters to try different working scenarios, the port can test and improve their operational resilience, such as working with increased cargo flows or limited physical assets.

Sophisticated simulation tools are available on the market via consulting companies, or simple level simulations can be built within a spreadsheet.

Almost any aspect of a port process can be simulated, from vessel movements to cargo operations, truck gate processing, and administrative tasks (Figure 6). The action of mapping and simulating the tasks leads to scenario trials and output results for cost, time, and quality improvements.

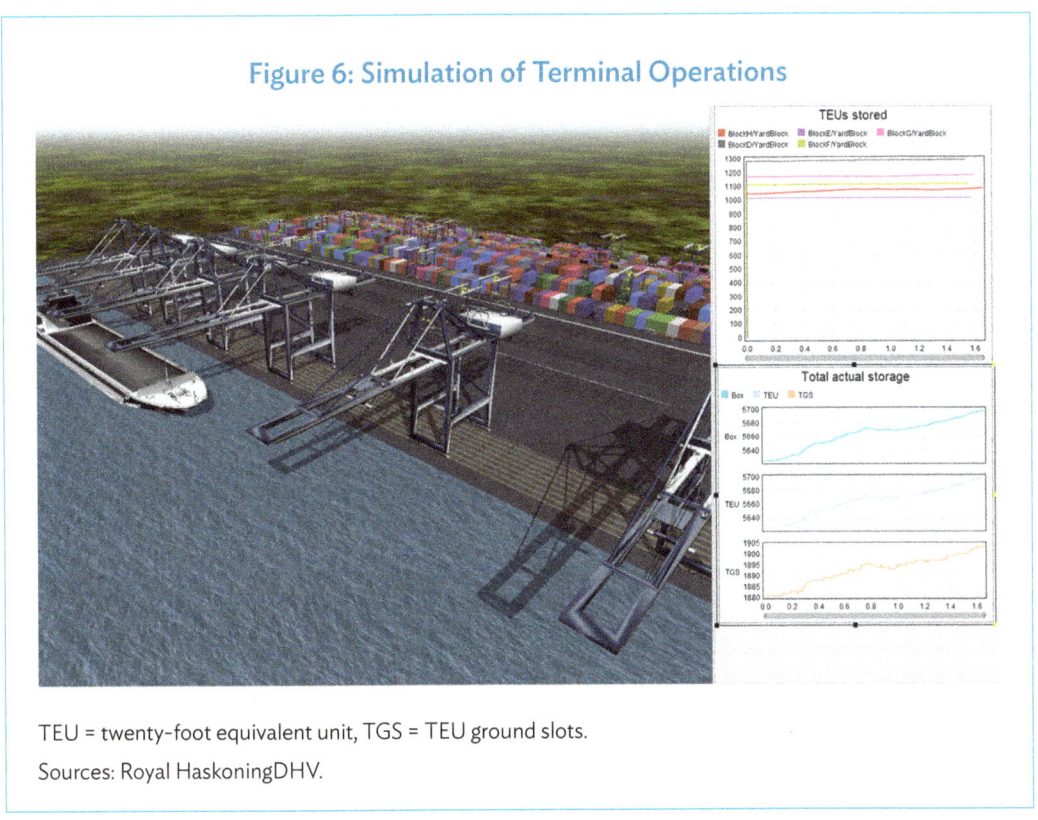

Figure 6: Simulation of Terminal Operations

TEU = twenty-foot equivalent unit, TGS = TEU ground slots.
Sources: Royal HaskoningDHV.

Digital Twin

A simulated model is limited in that it is only theoretical modeling of different scenarios. A digital twin moves beyond a static simulation and uses real-time data feeds from the port environment to create a working virtual model of the port facility. This may be only for a specific part of the port—such as a dry bulk conveyor system—or for the whole entity, or beyond the supply chain.

Having a digital twin of a facility allows the port to perform forward scenario trials more quickly based on real-life operations to guide fact-based decision-making with a predicted or trialed output (Figure 7). A digital twin also allows better-quality reactions when something changes in the process, such as a crane breakdown or vessel congestion, to predict the onward effects of each option that the port manager could decide upon.

The evolutionary process and learning exercise at this stage are fundamental to the ability to truly automate processes or equipment, where all key variables are mapped and understood, with parameters trialed virtually, before implementation on the port in real life.

Digital Transformation

The ultimate stage of smart port maturity is where port processes are managed by machines, removing daily tasks from human operators or managers.

This digital transformation usually focuses on particular areas of the port operation, either in administrative processes like invoice calculations or in repetitive physical tasks such as gate opening for security access.

Figure 7: Digital Twin in Logistics Industry

Source: Royal HaskoningDHV (Lanner).

The aim of automation in a port environment is to improve overall efficiency, with added benefits of improved safety, greater predictability and reliability, and cost-effectiveness.

The flagship projects of container terminal equipment automation may not provide immediate greater productivity in comparison with manual operations. However, they will improve over time and can be suitable for particular global markets.

For smarter ports, the principles of automating processes or tasks can be applied at a lower level, with more feasible investment and business benefits.

The understanding of the port functions gathered in the previous stages will allow a quantifiable focus on issues impacting the business and will support a further push toward automated solutions in these focus areas.

Many multi-cargo ports are focused on automating processes by either enabling clients to control their processes (self-booking) or integrating systems and processes to reduce administrative efforts such as invoice creation or customs clearance processes.

Within complex processes, such as in large container terminals, automation and optimization tools are used to schedule container movement tasks based on the location of terminal tractors to minimize empty traveling distances.

The elements of smart port maturity come together to make the whole port smarter, from planning and customer experience to cargo handling, security, and safety.

2.4 Examples of Smart Port Initiatives Worldwide

An inexhaustive list of projects in the sector around the world is provided in this section to illustrate the range of strategies and solutions available in this constantly evolving sector. The list ranges across the key sectors of smart ports and represents activities at each stage of the path to smart port maturity. The step related to the path to smart port maturity is indicated for each activity.

Operational Efficiency (Step 2 Collaboration, Step 3 Decision Support)

Cargo tally in field operations. Cargo tallies are used for digitizing information on cargo status. The data are connected through apps to provide real-time information to port operators and consumers, thereby promoting enhanced customer service experience, predictability of cargo release time, and port operating efficiency.

Multi-cargo and small port terminal operating system. Terminal and vessel operations performance can be measured using a centralized terminal automation system or terminal operating system (TOS). Similar to the Caribbean islands, where local port authorities have adopted specific software designed for small port multi-cargo operations, the Pacific islands would benefit from a software licensing and delivery model, remotely hosted (i.e., in the cloud) to minimize the need for local IT infrastructure, unlike traditional TOS hosted on local servers.

Port community portals. Port community portals can be used to operationalize the single window concept to promote trade facilitation (i.e., a one-stop-shop portal for importers and exporters) (Figure 8). The creation of centralized customer portals provides a one-stop-shop to facilitate all interactions between traders with the port and its regulatory bodies (customs, etc.) to share data and automate administrative processes. Maqta Gateway of Abu Dhabi Ports in the United Arab Emirates is a good example of collaboration and the benefits of digital transformation within a supply chain. This system captures customs declarations, duty payments, port service bookings, trucking, and vessel scheduling all within a shared platform environment.

Equipment remote control. It involves unmanned and remote control container terminal equipment, removing staff from dangerous working areas and permitting multiple machine operations from a single remote control station. At Maasvlakte 2 Terminal in the Netherlands, all cargo handling equipment in the terminal is unmanned with remote control supervisors in a central office. It reduces workforce but requires a significant investment in equipment and specialist IT solutions.

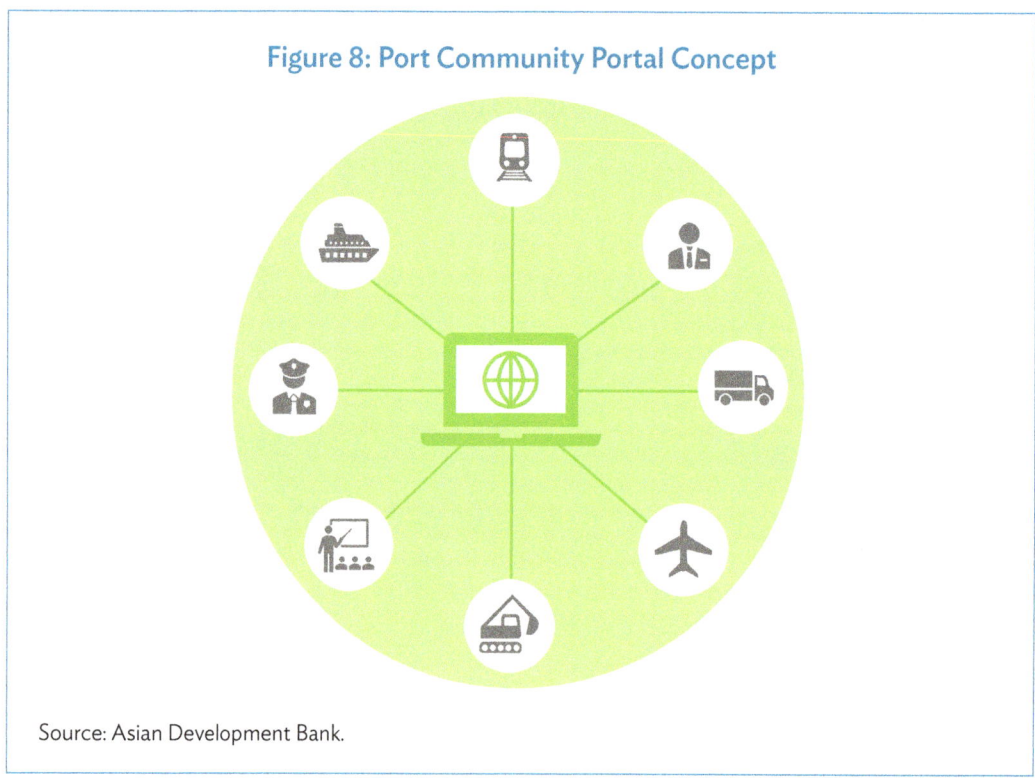

Figure 8: Port Community Portal Concept

Source: Asian Development Bank.

Remote control station. (photo by © kosta_iliev / Adobe Stock).

Asset Management (Step 1 Data Capture, Step 5 Digital Transformation)

The monitoring and maintenance of, and future investment in, port assets are key elements to efficient terminal operations and need careful attention to ensure that the availability of port equipment does not become the bottleneck in the port.

Automated mooring. The use of automated mooring systems removes staff from the dangers of line handling and improves the speed of berthing and unberthing. These systems also enhance vessel stability in exposed berths by reducing roll and surge of the vessels, allowing greater cargo operational safety and better working conditions. Various technologies involving suction, magnetism, or physical attachments to bollards or quay aprons are used.

Automated mooring system. (photo from Cavotec. http://www.cavotec.com/en/your-applications/ports-maritime/automated-mooring/container).

Monitoring of equipment usage. Monitoring of equipment usage and safety is key to improving training and machine longevity. Real-time data feeds from equipment can be used to track path, stability, steering, engine alerts, and fuel usage. This activity allows managers to observe the best use of equipment and improve driver behavior and safety.

Business Resilience (Step 1 Data Capture, Step 4 Learning)

Many aspects comprise a stronger business resilience in ports, but these are all data-led and use simulation and forecasting to understand future events and the possible reactions of ports.

Digital twin. Singapore is developing a full digital twin for the entire city and its key infrastructure, including the port and the new mega terminal at Tuas. The digital twin will capture information from the offshore and onshore supply chain, enabling modeling and scenario testing to ensure operational safety (Figure 9). For example, in case a new and bigger vessel is expected to visit the port, the digital twin can be used to verify that the vessel can be maneuvered safely to and from the berth. It may also identify under what conditions this new vessel is allowed to access the port.

Critical asset monitoring. Within ports, there could be many legacy assets that are owned and maintained by the port, often without a long-term strategy for investment. The addition of sensors and data analytics can improve the maintenance regime and guide future investment or replacement. For example, in the United Kingdom, a project is ongoing to design sensors and analytics to monitor the status of lock gates that were built in the 1920s (Figure 10). There are concerns about the technical capacity of the asset, and it is difficult to decide on the preferred maintenance regime without measured data.

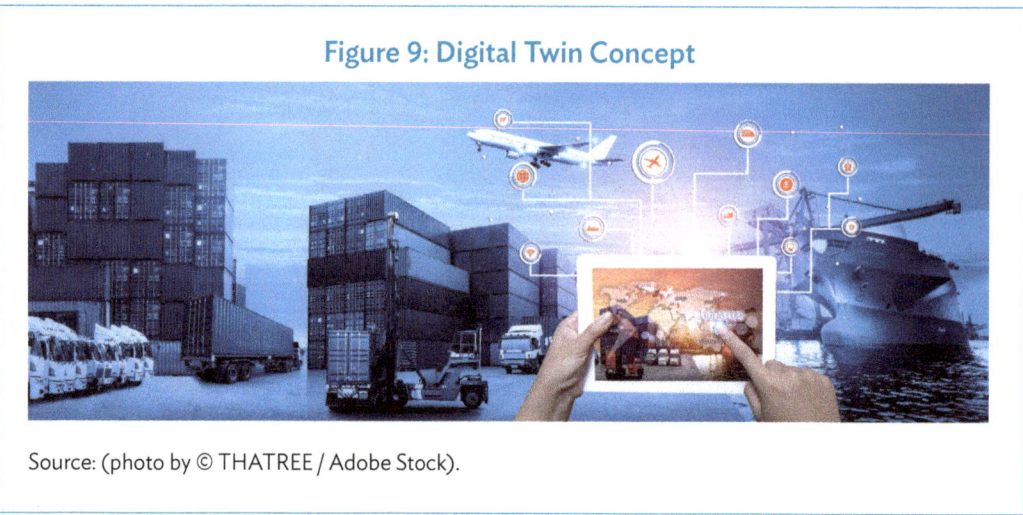

Figure 9: Digital Twin Concept

Source: (photo by © THATREE / Adobe Stock).

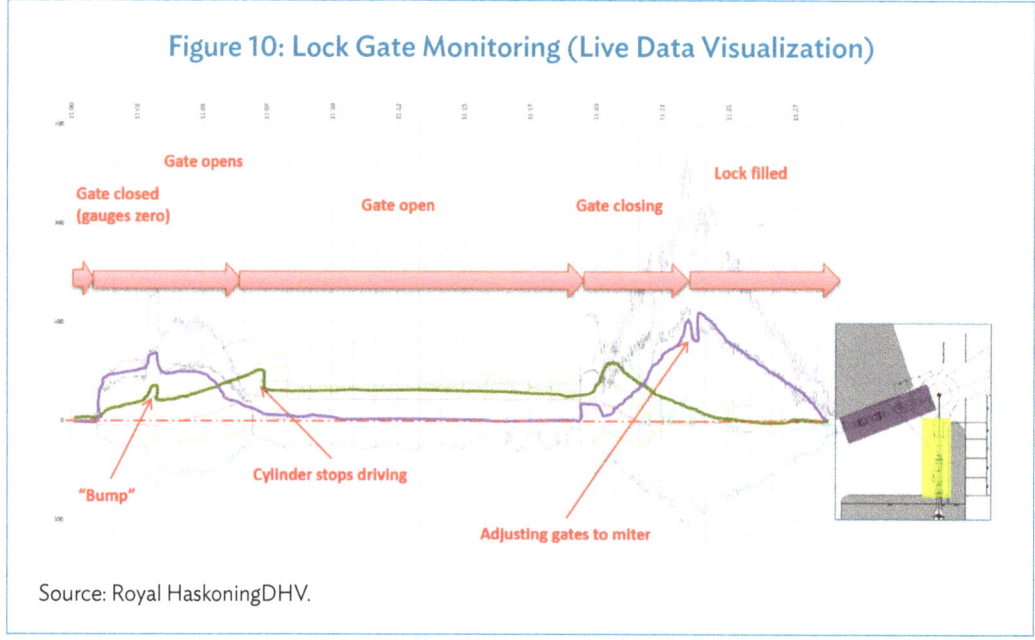

Figure 10: Lock Gate Monitoring (Live Data Visualization)

Source: Royal HaskoningDHV.

Safety and Security (Step 1 Data Capture, Step 2 Collaboration, Step 3 Decision Support, Step 4 Learning)

Closely linked with business resilience is the need to actively manage work safety and site security within a port. A successful port facility is both safe and secure. Smart ports can boost safety and security through technology tools.

Gate and access automation. The automation of access control and cargo entry and exit is a common tool in container terminals and growing for mixed-cargo ports as a whole. Automated gates can check driver and vehicle identities (with optical character recognition cameras and RFID tags) and cargo receipt or release (with optical character recognition) to automate the human processes carried out by security and port gate staff. These systems capture images of cargo condition and vehicles plus drivers for security monitoring and cargo claims. Integration with a TOS or port community system is typical.

Gate control. (photo by © zatevakhin / Adobe Stock).

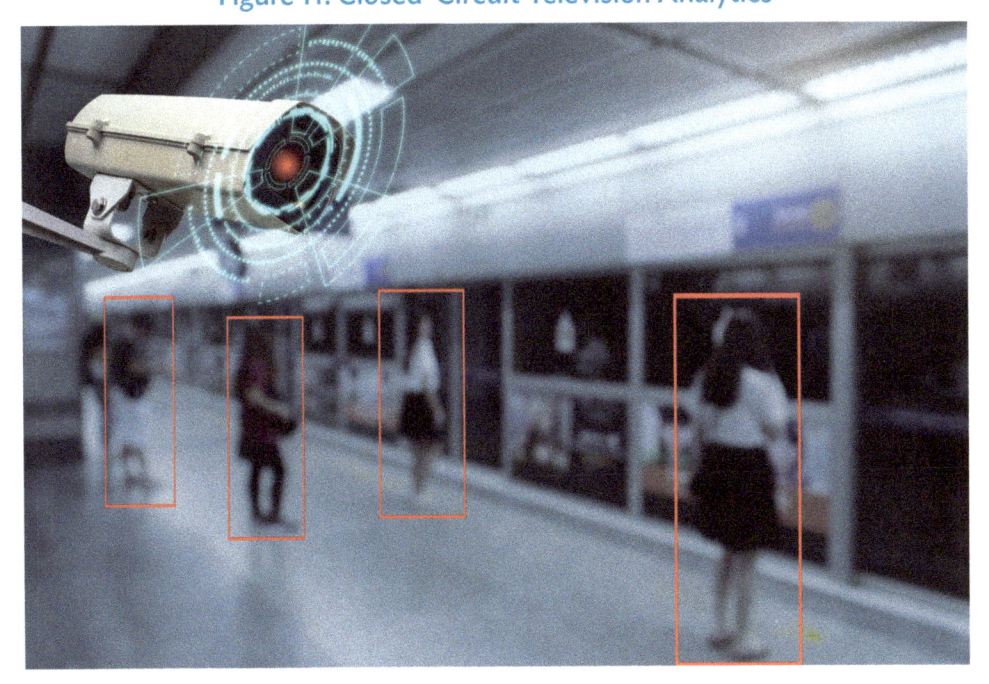

Source: (photo by © Vittaya_25 / Adobe Stock).

Intelligent CCTV. The use of closed-circuit television (CCTV) can be greatly enhanced by intelligent analytics to identify operational and security events, reducing the need for human supervision and improving accuracy and alerting capability (Figure 11). The operational data can be used to feed into congestion management or safety to capture staff behavior or location, or for perimeter protection. Intelligent CCTV has been used widely in different sectors and has proven to be a valuable source of data collection and safety improvement.

Energy Efficiency (Step 1 Data Capture, Step 2 Collaboration, Step 4 Learning)

Managing operations and processes with a smarter approach can improve resource and energy efficiency. There are some key areas where a specific focus on energy usage is used in the spectrum of smart ports.

Application for vessel scheduling and emissions monitoring. Sharing data on a common platform enables better decision-making, and simple calculations can provide port users information on potential energy or fuel savings. The Pronto community portal at the Port of Rotterdam is a recent example, where the focus on saving fuel for port users is being realized. In this case, the owner of the portal is the Port of Rotterdam, which provides customer service to vessel operators. The portal helps vessel operators to adjust vessel arrival timings according to the real-time berthing status at the port, enhancing vessel operating efficiency and reducing carbon dioxide emission.

Electrification. The trend in smart ports development is moving away from carbon fuels (mostly diesel) to electrified equipment, which is important to improve the local environment around the port. This trend reduces overall greenhouse gas (GHG) emissions. Electrified equipment is easier to control, and it monitors power usage, which is an essential element in overall efficiency considerations. For cost-efficiency, this improvement is taken when upgrading equipment or machinery. In regions with less-reliable power infrastructure, electrification should be considered within a wider strategy.

Backup power system. In some countries, having an on-port power backup supply is vital to maintain business resilience. Power can be produced from diesel generators (traditional approach). However, there is a growing interest in industrial battery storage for backup power for electrified equipment (particularly quay cranes). This system is also often combined with local power generation.

Environmental Management

Alongside energy efficiency, environmental management is the overarching need to reduce the environmental impact (sea or air pollution) of all port operations, either locally or globally. This system can be implemented all over the port, from managing lighting and buildings to optimizing vessel movements.

Energy-efficient terminal lighting. Conversion from traditional sodium lamps to LED lighting across all industries is common. In port areas, with large areas to provide safe lighting, there are notable energy advantages. Most new facilities have LED lighting, and many ports are working on conversion projects.

Renewable power generation. Ports are often landlords of large areas of land, presenting opportunities for the installation of renewable energy sources such as photovoltaic panels or wind turbines. These opportunities can generate local and emission-free power for port equipment, or provide revenue from sales to the national grid. This initiative is particularly valuable in the Pacific region where power generation relies on imported carbon fuels (coal, oil, gas) and where energy resilience can be improved by enhancing local power generation.

3. Relevance of Smart Ports Concept to the Pacific

While the benefits of smart ports concept are more prominent to larger ports, the applicability and cost-effectiveness of such sophisticated systems in the small island ports in the Pacific region are less known. The purpose of this section is to discuss the unique challenges in the Pacific in terms of regional characteristics and common port operational and logistical obstacles. This uniqueness forms the context in which the smart ports development framework has been established.

3.1 Regional Characteristics

- **Remoteness.** Given the geographical isolation from major international markets, maritime connectivity is critical to the economy, which heavily depends on agricultural exports and imports of basic commodities. Ports in the Pacific region also tend to operate independently with limited communication and coordination between port authorities. Transportation costs are high due to inefficiencies in the logistics system. Remoteness also results in costly operations in securing spare parts and maintenance for core assets.
- **Low cargo volumes.** Most of the cargo relates to import. There is only limited export from the region. The volumes are low and linked to local consumption (fuel and food). Several feeder lines operate in the Pacific islands. Australian and New Zealand ports are oftentimes used to transship from, e.g., Brisbane and Auckland to the feeder lines. The feeder lines then have a fixed route and drop cargo off at every port of call. There is little international transshipment in the Pacific itself, although Fiji (Suva) is trying to position itself in that role, the same as the Papua New Guinea ports. The main problem is the available draft that prohibits the use of larger transshipment vessels in these countries. There is domestic transshipment, as most countries consist of at least dozens of islands. The low economies of scale contribute to costly operations and maintenance for Pacific ports.
- **Natural hazards.** The Ring of Fire in the Pacific region subjects the small island states to frequent volcanic activity, earthquake, and tsunamis. These natural hazards are exacerbated by impacts of climate change, bringing increasingly frequent extreme weather conditions. Such events often lead to disruption of port and vessel operations and have a large impact on the reliability of the logistics chain. Ports in the Pacific are the economic lifeline of the country, and they provide critical access to basic supplies and essential services in the aftermath of natural hazards.
- **Reliance on imported fuel.** Pacific island countries are heavily reliant on the import of petroleum, which comprises a large share of their imports. To mitigate fuel costs and climate change impacts, governments have stepped up efforts to scale up renewable energy projects. The large energy costs and increasing renewable energy efforts potentially create an environment that promotes the electrification of port equipment and the implementation of renewable power for ports. For example, relatively higher levels of sunshine in the region potentially present an opportunity for the utilization of

solar panels to drive cost-efficiency. Such mature technology and relatively lower cost of hardware, as compared with its initial introduction, offer a short payback period and high return on investment.

3.2 Port Operational Characteristics

Field visits have been conducted in some ports in the Pacific to explore smart ports potential for the unique port operational characteristics of Pacific island countries.[5] The following trends were found.

- **Multipurpose ports.** Pacific ports tend to be multifunction, requiring facilities to import not only containers but also general cargo, bulk (grain, rice, clinker), liquids (mostly petroleum products), and vehicles. Multipurpose ports in the Pacific tend to also serve fishing vessels and cruise ships, posing additional challenges for efficient and safe operations for passengers and cargo.
- **Low level of digital maturity.** Most activities are dependent on manual input and/or paper-based systems. The utilization of integrated IT systems to streamline and integrate port processes is limited.
- **Lack of standard operating procedures.** Standard operating procedures (SOPs) are often not in place, or at least not recorded. Staff generally seem to know what to do based on experience, but misunderstandings do happen, sometimes leading to unsafe situations and/or inefficient operations.
- **Reactive vessel operations planning.** There is no regional vessel planning system, and individual ports are not taking a proactive approach in terms of vessel planning, leading to seasonal delays and congestion when vessels arrive at similar times.
- **Customs and biosecurity operations as a bottleneck in the operations.** The main causes for delays in the customs and biosecurity operations are the generally insufficient personnel capacity and the labor-intensive and time-consuming procedures. Lack of suitable infrastructure to support the inspections (e.g., not all ports in the Pacific have container X-ray scanners) further lengthens the whole procedure.
- **Limited planned maintenance.** Maintenance is mostly ad hoc, and due to the lack of sufficient spare parts in the port, any equipment breakdown could lead to port downtime or reduced operational efficiency.
- **Labor-intensive procedures.** Overall, the visited ports are very paper-intensive with lots of built-in inefficiencies. Processes rely on the performance of individuals, rather than a well-working system. There is much room for streamlining and integrating port procedures and operations. For more developed ports with sufficient scale, there could also be potential for automation of certain processes. While such measures can enhance operating efficiency, training needs to be provided to existing staff for them to learn new skills in line with the new procedures and digital tools.
- **Lack of coordination among agencies and port users.** Different parties in the ports were mostly working in silos, without regular communications or connected systems, leading to duplicative work among agencies and long process times for imports and exports.
- **Potential for digitalization.** The logistics chain is a relatively self-contained system that is less influenced by external conditions due to the Pacific region's geographic remoteness.

---

[5] These ports include Queen Salote International Wharf in the Kingdom of Tonga, Honiara Port in Solomon Islands, and Suva Port International Terminal in the Republic of Fiji.

This remoteness presents an opportunity for the Pacific ports to move toward greater digitalization due to their low-level technical complexity.

- **Limited technical competency.** One of the main challenges in the port sector is technical competency within the workforce, worsened by the relatively high level of staff turnover. The smart ports concept can play a role in closing this gap. The use of smart technology can reduce reliance on physical labor and create higher-value jobs, providing a more attractive career path for port staff and potentially promoting better talent retention in the ports industry.

The table provides a comparison between the three visited ports in terms of the different levels of digital maturity across the region. The differences can be related to port size, port ownership, or even the entrepreneurship of individuals in the port management team. The sample size of visits is too small to generalize conclusions. What is clear is that there is no one-size-fits-all solution for the Pacific island countries. Individual assessments are needed to identify the pathway of each port to digital maturity.

Table: Observations per Visited Port

Observations	Queen Salote International Wharf (Kingdom of Tonga)	Honiara Port (Solomon Islands)	Suva Port (Republic of Fiji)
The port is the lifeline of the country as the single point of import of all goods and materials.	Yes	Yes	No
The port is run in a basic way with operations at a relatively low level of digital maturity, still requiring a lot of manual input, which is prone to errors and inefficiencies.	Yes	Yes	No
There are no written procedures for any of the port operations, which could lead to misunderstandings and inefficiencies.	Yes	Yes	No
A form of terminal operating system is being implemented, which helps define operational procedures and is used to drive a yard planning system and reduce paperwork.	Yes	Yes	Yes
Planning of vessel arrivals is very reactive, which could lead to congestion and vessel delays (note that this is a regional issue).	Yes	Yes	Yes
Security is at a low level of digital maturity, with some digital tools to manage access in and out of the port.	Yes	Yes	Yes
Planned maintenance is limited, leading to the reduced capacity of equipment (through breakdowns) and other assets, which impacts the port productivity.	Yes	Yes	Yes
Several energy efficiency measures have been put into place.	No	Yes	No
New equipment assets are not well maintained or operated by trained staff, which is likely to cause early machine wear and failure.	Yes	Yes	No

continued on next page

Table continued

Observations	Queen Salote International Wharf (Kingdom of Tonga)	Honiara Port (Solomon Islands)	Suva Port (Republic of Fiji)
Safety is compromised by staff working in the same areas where equipment is being operated without proper communication tools.	Yes	Yes	No
Shift gangs are relatively large, and productivity is difficult to manage, resulting in some built-in inefficiency for vessel operations.	Yes	Yes	No
Customs and quarantine operations are considered a bottleneck in the operations, leading to longer dwell times in the port than necessary.	Yes	No	No
Different parties that are active in the port hardly talk to each other or share information.	Yes	No	Yes
Port processes require a lot of paperwork, which is time-consuming and leads to reduced port productivity.	Yes	Yes	Yes

Source: Royal HaskoningDHV.

3.3 Applicability of Smart Ports Concepts

The main conclusion after the field visits is that some fundamental processes need to be put in place as a prerequisite for digital transformation in the Pacific. The operations at the visited ports require enhancement across the organization to raise the level of good practice, which is needed as a foundation to build further smart port solutions. These areas of improvement include the following:

- Implement SOPs within a quality management system to identify all port procedures and shortcomings. Tools such as business process mapping could be used to trace stages from the arrival of cargo at the port to the delivery of that cargo to the end user.
- Establish a safety management system to support the creation of safe systems of work and risk assessments for the port operations. These tools will be used to train staff in their tasks (operational, safety, environmental).
- Train and certify port staff on the safe and productive use of cargo handling equipment, lifting, and lashing operations.
- Create more health and safety awareness by introducing toolbox safety talks before every operation.
- Capture health and safety incidents in the safety management system with monitoring and remedial action reporting including disciplinary actions.
- Create an asset management system to understand port equipment usage and manufacturer-recommended maintenance schedules. Stocks of common spare parts should be acquired and suitably stored to improve equipment availability.
- Consider improvements in procedures and regulations in customs and biosecurity to reduce cargo inspection and processing but provide adequate resources to deliver the procedures effectively to minimize the impact on the nation's trade.

In parallel to these procedural and practical recommendations, some technology initiatives can support the port to be safer, more secure, and cost-efficient with improved cargo handling. Below is an overview of typical smart port solutions with some views on its applicability to the Pacific context. These solutions can be applied to different stages of the port's digital maturity journey.

- **Energy efficiency.** Technology to improve energy efficiency, and thereby reducing operational costs and environmental impact, applies to the Pacific to some extent. Solutions like solar or wind energy can be easily implemented as well as LED lighting for the terminals. Solutions such as equipment electrification and/or the provision of shore power[6] seem more difficult to justify given the relatively low number of vessel calls and low volume of cargo handled in the region.
- **Operational efficiency.** There are opportunities to improve operational efficiency using new technologies in the Pacific region. Complete automation of (container) terminals seems a bridge too far in view of the low transport volumes, but implementing digital systems to measure performance and identify bottlenecks in the port operations seems very much relevant in the Pacific context.
- **Smart asset management.** Smart asset management is applicable and can help reduce the operating expense in the Pacific, but the amount of investment and type of system selected should be in line with the complexity of the assets in the port. Any smart asset management system should be preceded by a thorough analysis of the critical assets in the port and what needs to be measured to make optimal use of these assets.
- **Safety and security.** Any technologies that improve the safety of individuals and cargo security can be applied in the Pacific. Investments in digital solutions should be in line with the target levels of safety and security. For example, a CCTV system may help supplement and improve terminal security and reduce the need for manual security rounds, particularly in hazardous areas. The need for additional motion detectors should also be assessed and weighed against previous security breaches and the need to retain staff as security officers.
- **Port connectivity.** The end goal of the implementation of smart port solutions is to provide meaningful data to enable informed decision-making by the port users. At the next tier, connectivity between different ports in the Pacific could bring down transport and logistics costs for the region. An initial step in this process could be the development of a regional vessel arrival system with predictive capabilities to advise shipping lines on the best route to take. This system could then later be expanded by introducing the rest of the logistics chain in the Pacific region.

---

[6] Shore power is the supply of electrical power from the shore to the ship when its main and auxiliary engines are shut down.

4. Smarter Ports Development Framework

A smarter ports development framework has been established to encourage the piloting of smart ports concept in less-developed regions, particularly the broader challenges of ports in the Pacific. It is important to recognize that each port is unique and has specific characteristics posing distinctive challenges for its growth and development. Therefore, this report does not intend to promote a one-size-fits-all approach. The appropriate level of smart port maturity and sophistication should be designed according to the individual needs and scale of each port. The framework and suggestions can be scaled according to the size of individual ports.

4.1 Regional Mission and Vision

An initial proposal for smart ports mission and vision statements has been developed for the region to facilitate strategic discussions among decision makers. These statements are useful tools of strategic planning, and they can best be described as a compass (mission) and destination (vision) of the sector. The mission statement provides a clear and effective guide for making decisions, while the vision statement ensures that all the decisions made are properly aligned with what the individual ports, as well as the port community, hope to achieve. The proposed definitions below can be used as a good starting point to design the smart port initiative and should be adjusted according to the specific needs of each port.

Four broad thematic areas have been identified to support the mission and vision statements, taking into consideration ADB's operational priorities in ADB's Strategy 2030 and the unique development characteristics in the Pacific region (Figure 12).

Smart Ports Mission Statement for the Pacific

"To implement relevant and proven smart technologies in existing ports to improve operational efficiency and business reliability, increase resilience and sustainability, and enhance regional cooperation and integration"

Smart Ports Vision Statement for the Pacific

"To enable a transparent port logistics sector working together as one region and one port community to ensure best value for their customers at a minimum waste of space, time, money, and natural resources"

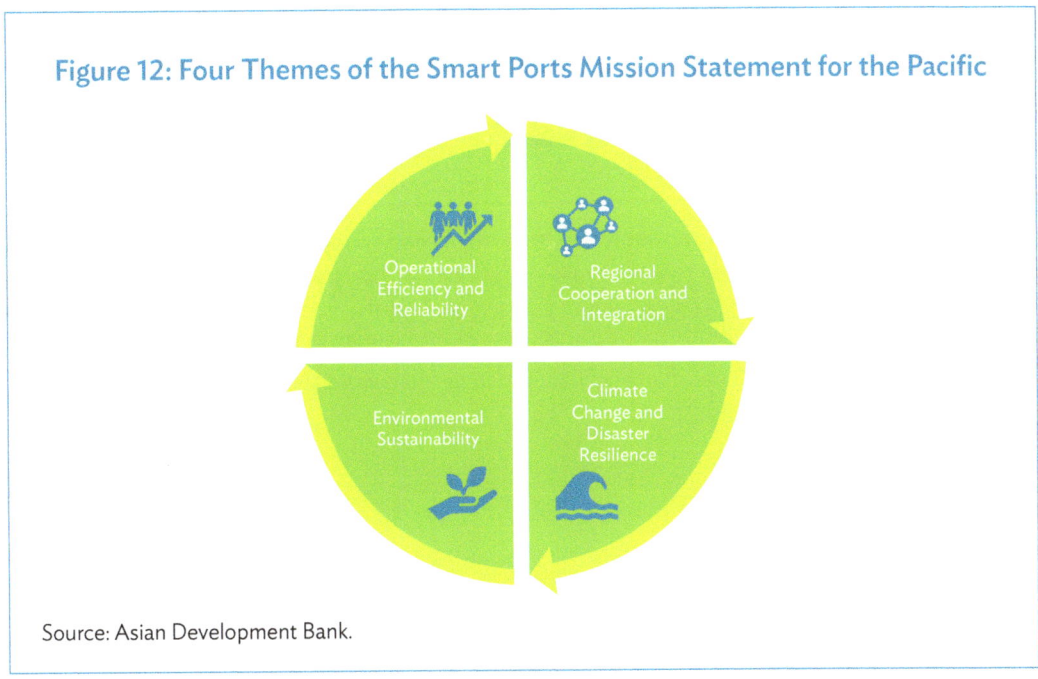

Figure 12: Four Themes of the Smart Ports Mission Statement for the Pacific

Source: Asian Development Bank.

- **Improving operational efficiency and reliability.** Port terminal operating systems (TOSs) founded on well-defined working processes can help improve efficiency and safety, as well as reduce inefficiencies and fraud. SOPs should be established across different port users, stipulating clear roles and responsibilities in each process. All asset- and equipment-related data can be tracked in terms of performance and use to enhance reliability. This tracking can facilitate predictive maintenance. Security, especially cybersecurity, will become an important part of the business continuity, as all data are cloud-based and access should be restricted and protected.
- **Promoting environmental sustainability.** Environmentally sustainable solutions should be promoted to minimize the environmental impact of port operations. Regularly measuring and publishing greenhouse gases (GHGs) creates awareness of promoting greener operations and low-carbon growth. Mitigating harmful emissions can be achieved with equipment electrification and shore power that allow vessels to shut off their engines when inside the port. The potential of solar and wind energy, which is particularly relevant in the Pacific context, should be maximized to deliver more carbon-neutral operations.
- **Enhancing resilience to climate change and natural hazards.** The Pacific region has specific challenges when it comes to climate change and natural hazards, such as typhoons, earthquakes, and tsunamis. These events lead to disruption of vessel traffic and greatly impact the reliability of the logistics chain. With the right weather data and prediction models based on artificial intelligence, port authorities can be alerted promptly to potential threats to the port and its operations. Based on such information, disaster preparedness and response plans can be put in place to proactively mitigate impacts.
- **Strengthening regional cooperation and integration.** Cross-border infrastructure needs should be addressed to strengthen the region's participation in global value chains. There is scope to introduce advanced technology and streamline customs processes to enhance border security and promote trade facilitation. In maritime operations, flexible routing should be encouraged in lieu of the stringent vessel routing, which is the current practice. There is much to gain in terms of reduced logistics costs in the region through

more coordination and cooperation between the different Pacific ports. Current port tariffs in the region are relatively high as compared with the rest of the world. The lack of coordination brings about limited efficiency, which increases the operating costs. Port tariffs are expected to decrease with enhanced efficiency of port operations and closer cooperation between port authorities.

The next sections provide more details on the thematic strategies to initiate smarter ports development goals. It is crucial to determine targets or key performance indicators to monitor the progress against each strategy selected and the overall theme to help bring focus on the improvement areas that the port management wants to achieve. Such key performance indicators will also support in deciding on what processes to measure and what tools and sensors to purchase to measure performance.

4.2 Smarter Ports Thematic Strategies

Theme 1: Improving Operational Efficiency and Reliability

Improving operational efficiency is not simply a matter of implementing new technologies. Without proper standardization and systematization of the port processes, there is nothing to automate. Therefore, an important early step should involve mapping of all business processes and simplifying work procedures to optimize workflow. Improvements can be supported by implementing a TOS.

The reliability component of this first theme relates to business continuity. Smart asset management plays an important role, as equipment breakdown is one of the main contributors to reduced productivity in the ports. Communication system and advanced security systems can deliver more reliable and predictable port operations. Below are some examples.

Terminal Operating System
In a modern container terminal, a TOS is typically deployed as a tool for record-keeping, planning, and control purposes. The TOS serves and is served by port staff and potentially various port users such as shipping lines, truckers, regulators, and analysts.[7] It could be an upgrade of any existing system or current TOS. In case the existing cargo mix and relatively low volumes do not support a specialist container TOS, a multi-cargo and port-wide system can also be valuable in improving port operations by incorporating a broad range of port functions. The TOS could support:

- vessel booking/scheduling;
- berth planning;
- marine resource usage (towage/pilotage services);
- cargo manifests;
- consignee/customs status (red, orange, green);
- import/export of Automated System for Customs Data (ASYCUDA) message formats with the customs systems;
- cargo operations monitoring—vessel tally (on a mobile device) and delays/events;
- yard storage locations;
- customs or quarantine clearance/inspection status;

---

[7] *Port Technology*. 2013. Terminal Operating System Selection. 24 July. https://www.porttechnology.org/technical-papers/terminal_operating_system_selection/

- port services such as stripping of cars or fumigation;
- truck entry/exit and cargo collections/deliveries;
- calculation of billing for services performed at the port; and
- automated report production for agent needs.

The expansion of the TOS into all these areas will require refinement of the port processes (quality management) and adoption by all the stakeholders and port users to make it effective and for the benefit of all parties. The TOS is the core of modern port operations to build further improvements, as it provides data capture and management platform, enforces standard processes, and delivers clear and shared performance data for mutual improvements over time.

A key element of TOS implementation is real-time input by each part of the process, which requires mobile device usage for vessel tally and yard locations particularly. The expense of Wi-Fi networks may be avoided through the use of cellular phone data networks, providing a more flexible and broader network with minimal running costs. For yard locations, it is recommended that the equipment operators perform the "clerical" tasks for better quality and real-time input to reduce the need for staff to access hazardous zones around reach stacker yards.

 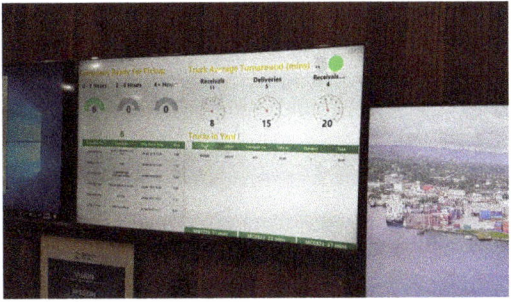

Sample terminal operating system. An initial terminal operating system is under implementation in Solomon Islands. (photo from Royal HaskoningDHV).

Semiautomated Gate Access

Rather than a fully automated gate, which is expensive, a semiautomated gate may be the better solution in the Pacific, which has relatively low traffic. By distributing RFID tags (swipe cards) to certified drivers and linking this gate access system to the TOS and security systems, the incoming and outgoing trucks and drivers can be monitored. This monitoring measures and improves turnaround time. Semiautomated gate access is already being implemented in Honiara Port (Solomon Islands) and can be easily copied by other ports in the region.

Automated Weighbridges

By introducing automated weighbridges coupled to truck identification tags, linking the container record information to the TOS, the containers are automatically weighed and registered. By doing this before and after truck visits to the port, the net weight of the container can be determined, fulfilling the obligations to declare verified gross mass for all export cargo. This strategy is also relevant from a road safety point of view (ensuring that maximum axle loads are not exceeded) for import containers and administrative point of view for any weight-based service billing.

Risk-Based Customs Management System

In most ports in the Pacific, the customs process is a bottleneck and the department is understaffed, leading to delays and congestion. Non-intrusive inspection equipment such as X-ray scanners will help speed up the customs process by using non-intrusive inspection practices and reduce the risk of fraud. These scanners are already operating in some ports and being procured in other ports, such as Apia in Samoa.

Smart Asset Maintenance

The use of smart machine sensors and data capture as inputs to a preventative maintenance scheme is an initial step that can be taken to improve the longevity of assets and equipment. This strategy may include fuel usage monitoring per machine, which helps to collect data in real time from equipment in terms of engine alerts and safety incidents (which can be traced back to individual drivers). The data collected can also be used to assess operational efficiency (e.g., moves per hour) and as input for identifying areas for improvement.

Another example is the global positioning system (GPS) equipment tracking, which will monitor speed, acceleration, deceleration, and overall driving distance. This information can be used to improve safer driving behavior of operators.

A final example is the smart fender, which records the number of impacts by vessels and the amount of energy dissipated. This will not only allow for preventative maintenance planning but will also help plan fender rotation (i.e., swapping highly utilized fenders with fenders that have a low utilization) to maximize longevity.

Intelligent CCTV

A useful security measure is the use of CCTV with intelligent alerting, e.g., CCTV with night vision and heat sensors or people recognition software. These state-of-the-art tools will reduce the need for visual inspections by security staff and provide more continuous and more accurate security support than by humans.

Improving Safety

In a mixed-use port with many machines and people working in a confined area, the risk of collision with ground staff is potentially high, particularly for reach stackers and large forklifts with limited visual range. The use of active RFID tagging on workers and machines to create proximity alerts can be an effective way of alerting drivers to the location of workers on the ground to avoid accidents. The creation of no-walk zones in heavy machinery areas can also improve safety and machine productivity.

A low-threshold incident reporting system for safety and environmental issues should also be implemented and promoted by management. This is as much a technology solution as a human solution and will require a change in working culture, which is usually more difficult to establish than implementing new technologies.

Faster Internet

The reliability of internet connectivity is a major risk in the Pacific, especially when ports get more digital in their operations. One solution is the use of cellular phone networks, which is usually cheaper and more reliable—3G is already fast enough for smaller ports. For ground staff communication in the terminal area, a landside radio network, which is proven technology and robust, can also be considered. Crucial to the implementation of any new communication systems is ensuring that proper human resources are available to monitor, maintain, and support these systems. IT staff training is also vital for project adoption and success.

Safety risk in labor-intensive offloading procedure. Workers offload containers onto the apron, potentially exposing themselves to safety risk (photo from Royal HaskoningDHV).

Theme 2: Promoting Environmental Sustainability

The second theme is environmental sustainability, which involves reduction of carbon footprint and energy consumption in the Pacific ports, as well as broader environment issues such as marine environment, air quality, solid waste management, and noise pollution.

Greenhouse Gas Emissions Monitoring
The main GHGs in ports are from vessels at the berth with running engines and from any non-electric equipment active in the port.

Electrification
By changing from petrol-powered to electricity-powered port equipment, the carbon footprint reduces, especially if it is combined with sustainable sources of electricity, such as solar energy (see Renewables Power Generation). Shore power has the added benefit of minimizing water pollution caused by the vessel's engines.

LED Lighting
A good energy-efficiency measure is implementing LED lighting for the terminal, which cuts energy consumption significantly. An even better solution would be to introduce smart-controlled LED lighting with motion-sensitive lighting and zoned control, increasing work safety and reducing light pollution.

Renewables Power Generation
Solar power and, to a lesser extent, wind power are relevant sources of energy in the Pacific. In some Pacific ports, solar power is already being used, mostly for perimeter lighting and power generation for office use. Solar power can also be considered to charge battery-operated electric vehicles.

Theme 3: Enhancing Climate Change and Disaster Resilience

Climate change and disaster resilience involves enhanced adaptability to the effects of climate change as well as action plans needed to be put in place in case hazard events occur.

Real-Time Weather Data Analysis

By installing weather stations, supplemented by buoys to capture and measure waves and currents, ports can get a better insight into the weather conditions and the resulting operating conditions. Predictive automated mooring is a new software developed by Royal HaskoningDHV that combines all this information. With weather forecast data, the tool will help predict mooring loads and forewarn the staff when adverse conditions are expected.

It is also advised that weather forecasting or modeling is published and shared with other ports in the region, so that it can be used by all stakeholders to support their operations (e.g., for improved vessel routing).

Intelligent Mooring Systems

Intelligent mooring systems provide an alternative to the conventional use of lines to secure vessels along the wharf. These solutions are especially relevant in ports with operational limitations in high-swell (wave) conditions. In principle, two systems can be adopted. The first is the vacuum or magnetic pads system that removes the need for mooring lines altogether. The pads are connected directly to the ship's hull and dampen its motions. The second system is a hydraulic device connected to the mooring lines to ensure they always maintain constant tension. This constant tension prevents snatching of the mooring lines and results in reduced vessel motions. The benefits of these systems include a quicker mooring and unmooring time and reduced downtime at the berth. Also, the ship movements and line forces can be monitored, which is useful if coupled to weather data, as it can guide weather limitations to unloading operations.

Disaster Recovery Program

Finally, a disaster recovery program is to be prepared and periodically tested to ensure that all individuals mentioned in the program are aware of their duties and responsibilities in the event of a catastrophe. Examples of this program are automated alerting systems and a platform sharing information.

Theme 4: Strengthening Regional Cooperation and Integration

The final theme is regional cooperation and integration. There is much to gain from reduced logistics costs in the region through better coordination and cooperation between the Pacific ports. The current freight rates are very high, which can be lowered through better communication between port authorities.

Slot Sharing by Vessel Operators

One opportunity is slot sharing between vessel operators for load balancing. This strategy will optimize the number of vessel-kilometers, but will require support or buy-in from the vessel operators. An online customer portal would make the whole booking process much more transparent, leading to lower costs and more efficient vessel schedules.

Sharing of "Grey Boxes" (Empty Containers)

Another strategy is the implementation of the "grey box" principle: this considers that all empty boxes (containers) are the same and can be shared with different vessel operators, which reduces the time to load these boxes onto the vessels. Since the efficient export of empties in the Pacific region is one of the main issues that needs to be solved, sharing of grey boxes can be a particularly interesting solution. This system needs buy-in from the vessel operators and box owners, which may take effort, but it has been successfully implemented in other parts of the world (mostly in Europe).

Regional Vessel Schedule Monitor

Regional vessel schedule monitor allows ports to focus resources on known port visits and to work around with other ad hoc vessel calls, giving more structure and overall efficiency, which decreases the cost of operations for the port and the lines (again delivering a potential reduction in sea freight costs). Once a schedule of time windows is created, this can be monitored in real time using vessel-tracking tools and a shared platform for ports to observe and re-schedule port calls where needed. This system could even be made smart by suggesting changes to the shipping route in case congestion is expected at a certain port. A potential app for such a system could work as follows:

- using automatic identification system data to plot all vessels in the region in real time;
- showing berthing windows at ports of call, with estimated variance for vessel call;
- estimating port call hours based on cargo exchange for the call;
- predicting congestion and delay based on anticipated routes and expected arrival times of the individual vessels and weather forecasts in the region (e.g., typhoons and storms);
- calculating costs of re-routing vessels based on preset costs of fuel, additional sailing time, etc.;
- advising shipping lines to change the route of a specific vessel; and
- sharing transparent information to all ports on this service.

Integrated Terminal Operating System

If customs and biosecurity could work with an extended TOS, then it may be feasible to use this platform to share and communicate manifest data to allow pre-arrival clearance of cargo for low-risk consignees, for example, removing vessel delays. This system could benefit small ports where sharing system platforms is very cost-effective and the Automated System for Customs Data (ASYCUDA) formats are industry standard.

The TOS would include all port operations such as those in the customs and biosecurity departments. The TOS could then also be expanded to include importers and exporters to act as a wider port community system for data exchange and cargo workflow.

Given the complexities and multi-stakeholder environment involved in customs, it may be unrealistic to expect to see a fully integrated system implemented overnight. Instead, an incremental process is recommended to use the TOS as a means of sharing information and promoting interagency communication. Such improved transparency would bring about greater efficiencies that should translate to a reduction of time and cost of cross-border trade, thereby improving the overall competitiveness of Pacific's trade with the rest of the world.

Smart "Quick Wins"

Some specific smart quick wins that can be cost-effectively implemented in the short term for the visited ports can be summarized as follows:

Improving Operational Efficiency and Reliability

- **Intelligent CCTV.** Invest in intelligent CCTV with motion detectors within specific areas to support the security department and reduce the need to do hourly inspections.
- **Automated weighbridges.** Semiautomated weighbridge linked to TOS can improve road safety and, if exports increase, verify gross mass compliance.
- **Training and certification for equipment operators.** It is not exactly a typical smart solution but is still very effective. From the interviews during the field visits, it became clear that training of operators is not common and carried out regularly. A proper training program with official certificates will be key to ensure fewer accidents, better fuel consumption, and less wear and tear of the machines, which increases the life cycle of equipment and protects the port's investment.

Promoting Environmental Sustainability

- **Smart asset management.** Implement smart asset maintenance to capture fuel usage per machine, either at fill-up (number of liters) or based on machine hours, to measure equipment usage and the operation's energy efficiency (e.g., fuel burn/units handled).
- **LED lighting.** Use LED lighting for the terminal to reduce energy use (potentially with smart features whereby only those areas in the port where operations take place are lit).
- **Renewables power generation.** Develop renewable power generation on-site to reduce the carbon footprint of port operations.

Enhancing Climate Change and Disaster Resilience

- **Real-time weather data analysis.** Apply real-time weather data analysis to capture live wind and precipitation data to share with port users. Further analyses could aid marine operations and vessel routing decisions.

Strengthening Regional Cooperation and Integration

- **Regional digital port community.** Collaborate on common challenges to reach economies of scale for these Pacific ports—e.g., cost-efficiencies of buying monitoring equipment in bulk, establishing shared portals, etc. Building on early successes, further collaborations can be made in the future to tackle more complex areas such as the port community approach to monitoring GHG emissions.

Becoming a Smarter Port—Challenges

The stages and options outlined above provide a general view of the concepts. The specific approach is variable for each port, depending on the particular cargo mix, location, challenges, and future business strategy.

As with any project, there are some risks and challenges in the implementation of the smart ports concepts, including

- standardization—business process, data collection, and system tools;
- integration of data—from proprietary and agnostic systems;
- return on investment—can be unclear for the short term;
- cybersecurity—a growing risk for ports that increasingly rely on technology;
- business flexibility—through the standardizing impact of automation (in some cases);
- collaboration and competition—difficult to collaborate where service or regional competition is high;
- people skills and resourcing—upskilling and restructuring organizations to benefit from technology;
- mixed stakeholder objectives—differing views from project owners affect clarity of vision;
- execution and business change—all technology projects can be difficult to deliver, particularly at the enterprise level; and
- change management—appetite by the management to improve operational conditions as well as the technical capabilities of port workers.

5. Getting Started

Many ports struggle with a practical implementation plan toward digital maturity. The final chapter of this report provides some guidelines on how to get started, which include suggestions for short- and medium-term strategies as well as key considerations in implementation. It should, however, be noted that each port is unique, and the implementation process may need small tweaks to make it most efficient for the situation in a particular port. Most of all, it should be acknowledged that there is no way back and that the port industry needs to get started soon. It is better to grow through challenges during implementation than continue business as usual.

5.1 Crucial Takeaways

The main messages that should be taken from this report by the reader are the following:

- **Any port can become smarter.** There is no limit in terms of port size for the implementation of smarter solutions. But this does not mean that all ports require the same level of smartness. Practical limitations prohibit most (if not all) ports from reaching an ultimate smart port level of maturity and sophistication. The journey to becoming smart can be made of many steps, a gradual process of transformation for the port to becoming smarter.
- **Start small, think long term.** Although steps to become smarter should be incremental, there should be a clear longer-term plan to make sure that any steps taken are in line with the longer-term perspective. One of the key pitfalls is to look at individual smart solutions in isolation, for the biggest results are achieved by integrating smart components into port operations and making them available for all. New partnerships may be needed, and collaboration between port users is crucial to maximizing the results of implementing cybersecurity, digitalization of port operations (including customs and biosecurity), and (semi)automated access to the port. It is recommended to pilot innovations and digital tools at a particular port to demonstrate proof of concept before it is rolled out to the wider region.
- **Gather data as a priority.** Data are key to developing smarter ports; therefore, any smart ports strategy should start with data gathering. A multiphase plan for smarter porter should be designed to ensure that the right data are collected with time-bound milestones, including the description of the necessary data to be collected at each stage. Such a description also includes procedures to ensure data quality assurance, safe data storage, software and hardware needs, and specifications for data collecting (including budgets).
- **Embrace change management.** As part of integrating new smart technologies into the port operations, reevaluating institutional and management structures in the Pacific will be needed. New roles may need to be introduced, and existing roles may become obsolete. Such change management may also involve strengthening regulatory and legislative frameworks, reinforcing interagency coordination, and enhancing transparency and accountability of the government and port authorities.

- **Focus on staff skills and safety.** Even though the smart ports concept is mostly about new technologies, people skills need to develop too not only to operate but also to maintain and improve these tools and systems to ensure sustainability. Last but not least, any smarter and more efficient port can improve operational safety by increasing operational clarity, automating port processes, and using better safety precautions in operations.

5.2 Tangible Short- and Medium-Term Strategies

Some smart quick wins and longer-term solutions can be implemented throughout the Pacific region, as mentioned in the four themes in Chapter 4. The main drivers for implementation will be the direct and indirect gains of these smart solutions, both monetary gains (e.g., a more efficient way of working) and nonmonetary gains (e.g., less pollution, disaster resilience). Bottlenecks will be the need to change the mindset of the people involved (e.g., reducing the workforce or changing skill set) and/or the costs of implementation. Figure 13 provides a list of strategies fitting within the four-theme framework, with an indication of quick win or longer-term solution.

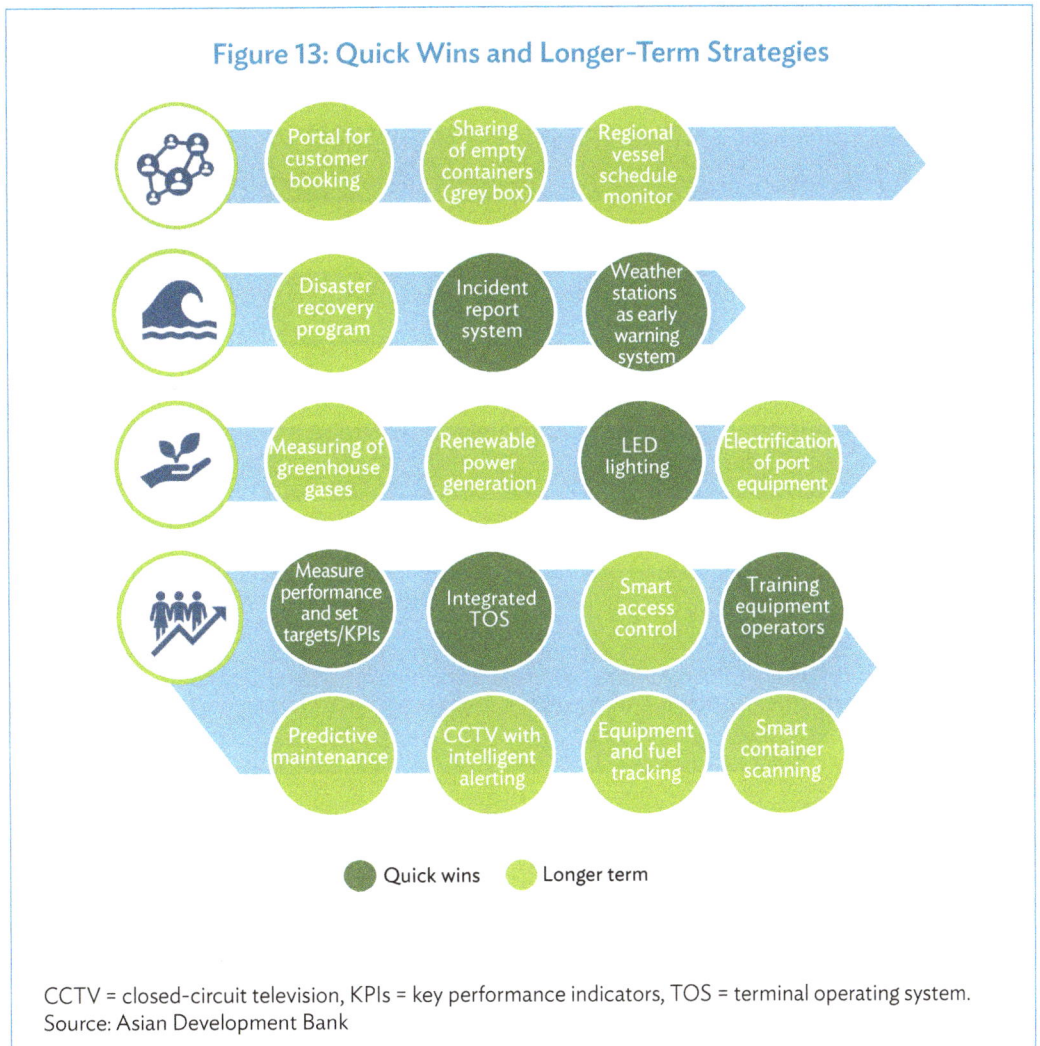

Figure 13: Quick Wins and Longer-Term Strategies

CCTV = closed-circuit television, KPIs = key performance indicators, TOS = terminal operating system.
Source: Asian Development Bank

It is recommended that ports work together and select feasible strategies so that implementation costs can be shared. A regional approach in smart port implementation can bring cost-efficiencies and catalyze smart ports concept adoption rates to achieve more sustainable growth as a region.

5.3 Key Considerations in Implementation

With the implementation of new digital strategies, some crucial issues should be taken into account. These issues are listed below and provide a road map toward digital maturity using small steps. Not all steps are relevant in all situations, but the main headings should always be considered by port authorities with a digital strategy.

- **Integration of Smart Components within Ports**
    - » Map business processes to understand key gaps, and repetition and causes of delay. Change practice to streamline operations, use software tools to automate, and share data where practical, but focus on cost or service improvements.
    - » Add networked or cellular-connected sensors to capture data from port infrastructure or operations (such as tide or weather information) and centralize data.
    - » Make best use of data produced from equipment or utility networks, bringing information together holistically for a real-time view of progress.
    - » Deploy stand-alone problem-solving solutions, such as access control.
    - » Integrate data sources for better collaboration.

- **New Partnerships**
    - » Capture a broader shared group to improve on common issues through developing partnerships of the following:
        - government bodies and port authorities for shared people, infrastructure, and regulatory issues;
        - shipping lines and trucking for resourcing, scheduling, and service levels;
        - equipment manufacturers for power/fuel and maintenance monitoring; and
        - information and communication technology and software vendors for the use of tool kit in remote or different environments.
    - » Collaborate with engineers and consultants to bring in new ways of working from international ports.
    - » Develop a port-led innovation hub concept that could work well to provide an open forum for problem-solving, ideally on a multi-island basis.

- **Piloting of Innovative Initiatives**
    - » Share problems and solutions across island ports to develop joint initiatives for a better return on collective investment.
    - » Identify key issues and be imaginative on technology that can help to solve the problem; being smart is about the deployment of existing and trusted tools into new environments or purposes.
    - » Select promising smart technologies for a specific port, then implement and test them. If they are successful, roll them out to the rest of the region.

- **Strengthening of Institutional Capacity and Governance**
    - » Create business change teams to enable growth and agility within the port structure, as people are key to success.
    - » Provide education and training on port practices and technology from other regions to give the staff tools and context to work on improvements.
    - » Provide training on technical skills, such as business process mapping, or on information and communication technology networks and data center management (with certification).
    - » Increase organizational value and focus on IT by investing in staff and resources.
    - » Create a vision and objectives for the port and embed these in all future infrastructure or modernization projects to keep moving toward the holistic goal. A smarter port is a task for all departments, not just IT-related.

- **Change Management**
    - » Establish a leading role for performance excellence within the port organization to cut across all departments, which is tasked to find improvements.
    - » Form focus groups within the port stakeholder community, as a change to practices or tools is only successful if everyone is supportive.
    - » Enable change with senior or governmental support for the overall vision and objectives.
    - » Develop an agile mindset to challenge traditional processes or structures.
    - » Form a regional working group to share ideas and improve cooperation. Most issues will be shared and, thus, sharing solutions is viable.